The Key to the Garden

 JOY AS A PATH TO GOD

SKYE LEITH

Skye Leith
PO Box 492
Nyack, NY 10960
thekeytothegarden@gmail.com

ISBN: 978-0-615-29604-3

You can purchase this book at www.thekeytothegarden.com

Published by Wondered Out Loud Press

Cover photo: Eileen's Mexican Sunflower by Skye Leith

Thank you, Eileen, Lazuli, Genevieve, Penny, Allan, Susan, Joe, Abe, and G. Fox.

The Key to the Garden

JOY AS A PATH TO GOD

For Mom & Dad

Christ spoke of a connection to God that is electrifying, miraculous and transformational, but the combination of time and institutions have gradually eroded His wisdom into little more than a set of rules. Living your life by rules can be tricky, because life does not usually deliver you simple problems that rules can adequately address. Wouldn't you rather ask God directly what you should do in every situation? This book will help you not only to rediscover the brilliance of Christ's explosive message, but to easily open up a living communion with God that you can access in every moment. The practical and relevant advice you'll find here will lead you through a road-map of the spiritual journey, point out common pitfalls, and give you numerous examples of how the mind works and how best to use it in service of the goal: hearing what God has to say and living a miraculous life by following that guidance. I do hope you'll get something from it.

Throughout the book, I use the term God and refer to God in the masculine, so we have a familiar language for our conversation. I don't think God is male, female, or anything you could ever find an adequate label for. Feel free to substitute the terminology of your choice.

There's more than one way to make hot sauce.

- G. Fox

The Good Father

My earthly father is a good father. When I'm happy, he's happy about that. If I ask him for something, he'll bend over backwards to give it to me. If I ask him for bread, he won't give me a stone, why would he do that? He's my Dad! He'll give me bread. Not stale bread, either - he'll give me the best bread he can find because he has my best interests at heart. When I'm enjoying myself, and when I'm healthy, Dad's happy. When I'm successful, not only is he happy, but he's proud, too. I think God is just like that.

If you are asking God for bread over and over, and seem to be getting a stone, you may be thinking, "Why isn't God helping me? He could if He wanted to. After all, He's God! Maybe I'm not praying hard enough, or maybe I'm being too selfish, asking Him for something just for me." Did you ever think about how our eyes, ears, and nose are aimed out instead of in? I think that's what confuses us sometimes.

How do you learn to hear God? A single phrase in the Bible points the way: *Love the Lord your God with all your heart and with all your soul and with all your mind.* You've probably heard and read that verse many times. But like many things in the Bible, it always seemed inscrutable. How in the world do I do that? I have a family to raise, a job to attend to, people tugging at me here and there, bills to pay. How does loving God unceasingly, with all that I've got going on, fit in to all that? And just as important, how would I know if I'm doing it right?

A clue to the answer is in how you feel. Let's say you open up your heart to God - should that feel good, or should that feel bad? It makes sense that the closer I am to God and the more I open up to His love and am loving Him, the better I should feel in my heart. It feels nice where God is.

If you disagree with the basic idea in that last paragraph, you probably won't get anything out of this book. I believe that being with God is never about suffering to prove your worth, or patiently enduring this horrible world until the Lord takes you to heaven where it's nice, or any ideas like that. Being with God is joyful! God is not punishing you or testing you. You don't need to be purified or cleansed, which doesn't sound like any fun at all. I'm not sure where those ideas came from, but don't think for a moment that God sees you as unworthy, and that living with God should be some kind of struggle or obligation that you must accomplish with stoic determination. Living with God is enormous fun, and you are more worthy to Him than the earth and the stars. If I'm feeling joy, it makes sense that I'm letting God in. If I'm feeling love for myself or others, it makes sense that I'm letting God in. If I'm feeling happiness and a zest for life, it makes sense that I'm letting God in. Conversely, if I'm feeling ornery, I'm closing down my heart and not letting Him in.

God is always there. His healing love and ability to help is always there, but if I'm not letting it in, that's not His problem, it's mine. Once I found that out, my own healing started. While I still lose my balance on a daily basis, I always know what to do to get back on board with loving the Lord above all else. When I do that, healing and everything else I could possibly want follow close behind. This may not make much sense to you right now if your body isn't feeling well, or your marriage is rocky or your kids are driving you over the edge. I know it's hard not to think about those kinds of things. But the day you make connecting with God your top priority, it will soon fall into place.

Joy Is Normal

When I tune into God's love, not only do I feel better, but I become His instrument, and I don't have to wonder any more about what to do with my life in general or at this very moment. When I tune into His love, I connect to His guidance and the path before me becomes clear. I'm not pulled any more this way and that by people and circumstances. I'm not guided by worry, guilt, fear or anger and the mistakes those emotions always lead me to. I'm led by Him, and being led by Him is the sweetest walk you can ever imagine.

Learning how to walk with Him is really simple to understand, but it does take a little practice. Children know intuitively how to do this, but as we get older we tend to get in our own way. In every moment, God is guiding us toward Him and we can tell by the way we feel. If I'm peeved at someone, that unpleasant feeling of being peeved is God gently telling me that I'm moving away from Him.

The problem is that we've grown so accustomed to being peeved, worried or guilty that we don't notice it feels bad - it's become a natural state of being. Feeling uncomfortable became ordinary and we accept that feeling bad is just part of being human. If we continue that pattern, the bad feeling naturally multiplies, and eventually makes us sick, and we become accustomed to that as well. Aches and pains become the norm. Paying close attention to the way you feel is an essential skill to develop if you truly want to align with God, because if we become accustomed to tolerating even subtle mental pain, this chronically separates us from God's clarity, and we unknowingly invite confusion and chaos into our life. How did we ever get it so twisted around? My heavenly Father wants me to experience joy, happiness, abundance and love right now, just as my earthly dad does. Once you learn to tap into God's joy, you are always at the well, drinking deep, and His well never runs dry. Anyone can learn how to do it. It just takes a small amount of sustained effort, much less effort than you would imagine.

Living close to God and becoming accustomed to hearing his guidance is not like buying a ticket to a movie, and once you're in, you're in. Being with God is something you have to consciously do, moment by moment. It takes some amount of focus in the beginning, but it naturally gets easier the more you do it. If you're like most people, one minute you're in alignment with God, then life presents you with a situation that causes you to drift a little bit away from Him and you have to consciously re-align again. This goes on your whole life, but with practice you can tip the balance of the time spent with Him versus the time you've drifted away so that you're with Him most of the time. Then life starts to get really interesting.

What's normal, if you walk with God, is joy. What's

natural, if you're in alignment with His will, is happiness. What's ordinary, if you're feeling His love, is energy, vitality and inspiration. This is not to say that we won't experience pain from time to time - the physical world has it's limitations. But even in the midst of pain, God has given me a choice about how I feel about it. I can feel pain and be worried, or I can feel pain and open my heart to an answer. I can feel pain and be afraid of it increasing, or I can feel pain and look forward to a healing. I can feel pain and become depressed, or I can feel pain and expect better days to come. Once I get a foot-hold in even a slightly better-feeling place, I know that my healing is on the way because in that place I know that I'm now standing closer to God, the Source of all healing.

Climbing the Ladder To Joy

You may have read studies about how loving feelings, even petting your cat, relieves stress and helps your body to heal. Science can label it what they will, but all I know is that when I'm loving God, loving others and loving myself, I feel good. When I feel good I know I'm on the road to healing. When I'm not feeling good, when I'm all bent out of shape about the government, or about that annoying person at work, or about how tight my shoulders feel, then I know I've got my back turned to God and I had better find something, anything, that will let me feel better and get me opened up to his healing love again or I'm in trouble.

God has never spoken to me audibly, but it doesn't matter because He gave us the ability to listen with our hearts. He lets me know, moment by moment, if I'm letting Him in or not, because when I'm letting him in, I always feel good, never bad. If I'm afraid, I'm not letting him in. If I'm angry, I'm not letting Him in. If I'm worried, I'm not letting Him in. Because fear, anger and worry really don't feel good at all. Why do we go to those bad feeling places? Habit, I suppose. Also, when the thing in my face is frightening, it's natural to be afraid. Let me qualify that - natural, but unnecessary, because we always have a choice about where we put our attention. God gave us that choice.

"Then you haven't felt the pain I'm feeling, because when this pain is hitting me, I have no choice and I can't think of anything else."

I hear that, loud and clear. We all know pain. But you've just got to hear this: if you're feeling fear, or anger or any of those bad feelings in your heart, you need to treat it like a big neon sign that says, *Now's the Time to Turn Towards God.* You can tell that this is true, because when you turn away from that fearful place, and back towards Him and his healing love, you feel better immediately, and gradually the fear subsides and the pain lessens, every time. When I feel that relief and loosen my grip, His love has room to come in. I keep His love out, He doesn't. He's always there, but if I don't get good at letting Him in, I may as well hunker down for a long hard ride.

With practice, we can choose to look at pain differently. Let's say that your son is involved with someone that you don't think is a good person, for whatever reason. I'm sorry it's painful for you to watch your son go down the road he has chosen, but you have to trust that God has the capacity take care of him. Remember this: If it feels bad, that's not God telling you he agrees with you that your son is making wrong choices, it's God telling you that you're drifting away from Him a little bit. Your son has his own connection with God, and he's the only one who can address it, just as you're the only one who can address your connection with God. Don't worry - God's got him covered. And when you start to get connected to God, the people around you will too, without you ever having to utter a word.

Sometimes the thing that has your attention can

be very big. Maybe you're worried about a frightening diagnosis, or you have a migraine that colors your whole world. At times like these, it might seem like you have no choice but to focus on the pain or fear, but there is always a way out. It may be a very small crack of a way out, but if you can find it, grab on. Look at it as a ladder. You can't reach the top rung from the bottom rung, but you can grab on to the next rung nearest to you. And the key is finding that next rung. Reach for it wherever you can find it. Maybe it's just taking a walk in nature, or maybe it's remembering your precious grandson's laugh, but God always gives us a choice. Find that next rung up and hold on for dear life, because it's the only way you'll be able to reach the next one up, and the next. If you keep on like this, in very short order you'll be at the top rung again, where God hangs out.

⚷   The Fast Track

If I want to get to a place where my heart is open to God's love, where do I start? If feeling joyful means I'm in God's vicinity, then I have to make feeling joyful my top priority. So the act of consciously looking only for the myriad ways God is blessing my life will in time expand into a white-hot communion with God. It may be hard to believe, but it really is that simple. If all you ever did was look for things to appreciate about God's awesome creation, and reside in that activity consistently, you'd be on the fast track to having a face-to-face with Mr. Big. Saint Paul gives us this key in Philippians 4:8: *Summing it all up, friends, I'd say you'll do best by filling your minds and meditating on things true, noble, reputable, authentic, compelling, gracious—the best, not the worst; the beautiful, not the ugly; things to praise, not things to curse. Put into practice what you learned from me, what you heard and saw and realized. Do that, and God, who makes everything work together, will work you into his most excellent harmonies.**

In other words, if I go looking for pleasant aspects about a situation or a person, I'll be able to find an unlimited number of good things that I could put my attention on, and doing that will invite God into my life. If I go looking for unpleasant aspects about that same situation or person, I'll be able to find an unlimited number of unpleasant things to consider. Intellectually, it's a complete no-brainer as to which path to take. In practice, it's less difficult than learning to play the piano. In other words, you can master it through repetition.

Getting into the habit of intentionally and consistently looking for only the positive aspects of whatever happens to have your attention is an attainable state of mind. Once we can comfortably reside in that state only a fraction of the time, it's downhill from there. Being consistently in that state over time builds until it generates an extraordinary state of joy, and since God is in the direction of joy, you see where this is going.

If that's all it takes to get to God why don't we do it? Besides just not knowing any better, I think one reason is that we're just not aware of how comfortable being uncomfortable feels. Low-grade, chronic pain somehow became the norm, and we expect ourselves and others to just suck it up and plow through, like tough pioneers roughing it all the way to Oregon in a covered wagon. It's practically patriotic to believe in the struggle! Then you feel justified in having a negative outlook when you're experiencing hardship, but ironically, it turns out to be the negative outlook that is the cause of the hardship, so it's a vicious cycle. Some people believe that getting to God has something to do with suffering, and that there's no fun in it. I guess the way I look at it, God would be thrilled for us to get to Him in any way at all, but would be doubly thrilled if it was fun for us getting there. The day you decide you're going to make it your number one job to look for things to appreciate and rejoice about, the hardship begins to soften, then dissolve, because it can't take the heat of the Presence of the Lord. Where God is, it is blissful. Where God is, it is fun. Where God is, you become 5 years old again on God's eternal playground where your only experience is joy.

What do you think being with God is like? I was never satisfied with any descriptions of heaven I heard in Sunday School. They all seemed so boring. Maybe it was the religious artwork that was misleading. From those images, it seemed like people in heaven did a lot of standing around praising God, which didn't seem like too much fun, especially if you had to do it for an eternity. Of course those old paintings were just a representation of the idea of union with God. The artist just left the good parts out of the picture. It is about praising God but that's not a passive act. I think you can taste heaven while you're living a full life right now, without that inconvenient death thing. Just kidding - death has got to be the most amazing ride imaginable. And if the little bit of heaven I can experience here is any preview of what's to come later, count me in.

Heaven is not in the direction of any painful thought. How could it be? When I'm worried or upset I can be sure that I won't run into God if I keep walking in that direction. God is only in the direction of joy. Joy is all that exists where God is, and you can choose to drink in that joy, or not.

⚷ God's Kung-Fu

If I'm angry, depressed, afraid, jealous or worried, the thing I've got my attention on may seem really important, but those feelings about it are a sure sign I've turned away from God. I can tell because those feelings never feel good, and when I'm tuned into God's love I always feel good. "But wait a minute," you might say, "what if I'm upset about this person who is doing this terrible thing? How can I ignore that?" If it's more important to you to be right than it is to be living close to God, that's your choice, but in my experience, being right always feels like hell. Heaven can be now, but that's your choice as well. God created you free, so you can choose either.

Let's go back to our verse again, *Love the Lord your God with all your heart and with all your soul and with all your mind.* Your primary responsibility in this world is that, and the verse says all your mind, not the parts of it you want to portion out to God. If you insist on keeping your focus on some misbehaving person, then the train has left the station - you've missed another opportunity to connect with God. Besides, do you really think God isn't capable of handling the people in His creation? That's like saying, "Look, Big Man, I know You created the earth, the stars, the sun and the moon, and the billions of galaxies spinning out into infinity, but I really don't think you can handle this. I better take care of this for you, God." Good luck with that!

Listening to God has got to become a full-time occupation if you want to be with Him now. Me, I'm not holding out for the hereafter, I want to be with God now, when it counts. Tomorrow will take care of itself, and unless I find a way to connect to God in this very minute, then my life here is being wasted. When I'm connected to Him, not only do I feel the bliss of His healing love, but then and only then is it clear what He wants me to do with my life. Until that time, I'm just flailing about here, like a fish out of water.

Being with God is like becoming a really cunning Kung-Fu master. You are just minding your own business when you are mercilessly attacked by a powerful enemy. Maybe a sickness, a bill you can't pay, a rascal who's making your life miserable, losing your job. Everyone around you thinks that you, Master Joy-Fun, are going to spin and give a head-kick to the enemy, but no - you walk up to the enemy, politely bow, and thank them for reminding you that they are temporarily distracting you from your number one job, which is being with God. So you assume your fighting posture and with lightning speed you scan your environment for something to appreciate. The enemy rises up and grows larger at this insult - so not only do you lose your job, but your health insurance! But you know that even canceled health insurance is no match for God's more powerful Kung-Fu. With quiet strength you quickly make lists of all the positive aspects of your life, and you find something to appreciate about your enemy - no matter how small. You even praise God for this perfect opportunity to hone your Kung-Fu. You look deep into the eyes of your enemy and say, "My mind has been mulling over what few good qualities you possess, and all the joyful thoughts I can muster on my own. My constant attention to these small, seemingly insignificant positive thoughts has multiplied them beyond measure. You are now outnumbered." God bursts forth like a million suns out of your heart and vaporizes your opponent! You bow, and return to your bowl of noodles.

If this were a movie, these are the words that I'd make with huge 3D letters that jump out at you: *To get to where God is, you have to make feeling joyful your top priority.* The easiest, quickest way to do this is to go through your day looking for reasons to absolutely burst into praise for God. If you're not finding things to praise God for, you're not looking. Rejoice about anything and everything you can find, and look forward to your connection to God improving. It will come sooner than you think.

Rascals

Now let's talk about all those infuriating rascals. They're all over the place, aren't they? Cutting in front of you in traffic, not cleaning up after themselves, not carrying their share of the load, raising your taxes, screwing up the environment, not treating us right, telling us lies! If it weren't for all those damn people, the world would be a better place, right?

I have a big shock for you. Are you sitting? Those rascals aren't the cause of your discomfort. Your separation from God is the cause of your discomfort. Because when you are aligned with God, you will always feel good, no matter what anyone else is doing. Do you remember that old Disney movie, Pinnochio? And how Pinnochio had a little sidekick, Jiminy Cricket? Well, Jiminy had it right: Always let your conscience be your guide. If you listen to your heart, God is telling you in every moment if you're loving Him or not. If you're mad at someone, you're not loving Him. If you're upset at the government, you're not loving Him. If you're annoyed that someone won't do what you want them to do, you're not loving Him. Feeling mad, upset or annoyed always feels bad in your heart, but that bad feeling is not because God agrees with you that those rascals are bad. That bad feeling is your signal that you've forgotten about Him.

Don't ever use someone else, and what they are doing, to separate you from God. It is never worth it. They may very well be doing something that is hateful or just plain stupid, but it's not my job to judge, or fix or correct them - God has that angle completely covered. My only job is to maintain an open, living, loving connection to God. And if I'm using someone else and what they're doing as my excuse to sever that connection, that would be my fault, wouldn't it? When you are in alignment with God and doing His will, you will always feel good.

What about the really, really bad ones - the terrorists, murderers and other evil-doers? When a baby is first learning to walk, her father never says, "Stop falling down, you stupid girl!" Her father knows that she's trying and so he encourages her, calling her to him again and again, no matter how long it takes. I think that's how our Father sees us. We keep falling, but He never stops saying, "Come this way, love, you're doing great. Keep at it, you've almost got it. It's going to be so great when you get this." No matter how bad we are at loving Him, He never gives up on us, and I can't believe that He ever gives up on the really bad ones either. What kind of Father would do that? He wouldn't say, "Hate to tell you, little guy, but you've run out of time! You couldn't figure out how to get to me quickly enough, so, sorry! Eternal Suffering and Torment for you!" Whether you agree with this or not, you have to let God handle these rascals because you need to get back to the business of connecting with Him. Jesus thought that connecting with God was so important that he dubbed it the greatest commandment. I'm with Him.

I had a heart attack about 5 years ago. I know now that the reason I got sick in the first place was because I had gotten myself pinched off from God's healing love. My world was chock full of all those infuriating rascals, misbehaving all over the place, and I kept tabs on all of them - what this one was doing wrong, what that one was doing wrong. And the 24-hour cable news cycle helped me to track them all! The angrier I got at them the more I closed off my heart - literally. It was such a relief when I realized that I don't have to judge another person, ever again. You have to trust that God is working with everyone, on His time, and He's got it all handled.

Sometimes, it's harder to navigate around those people who aren't overtly misbehaving, but who are caught in that place of worry and despair and they just have to tell you all about it. They have to tell you all about their unfeeling children, their cold spouse, their health issues, their bills, their long commute, their horrible job. Those people truly are in hell, but you just have to tell them, "I love you so much, but if I come down in that hole with you, then I'm not of any use to you, or me. I'm choosing to stay up here with God's love and when you're ready, we're both here waiting for you." You can also have this conversation with them in your mind, and it will have the same result. You'll get to stay with God, where it's nice, and from there you can see how best to help your friend.

Another really freeing thing about this is that none of those rascals have to do anything different for you to be with God. They don't have to change their behavior one bit. You may think that the only way you're going to feel better is if that rascal changes. So how is that going? I thought so. Everything in your world can stay exactly as it is today, and God will fix everything, but you have to take your attention off the rascal, and put it on God.

You are responsible for your connection to God, and that connection is sacred. That connection is your lifeline to every goodness you could possibly imagine. Don't ever let anyone or anything threaten that connection. You just have to be who you really are, and you are a child of God.

Getting Angry at God

Some of the most painful times of my life I experienced when I was chronically depressed. When you're depressed, you feel powerless, hopeless and helpless. You feel trapped in a box, unable to connect with other people or to any good feelings at all. While it may seem that God has abandoned you, this is impossible because God is always present. His power, capability and unconditional love are always there, but when you're depressed you can't see Him. Turned in on yourself, the hollowness there can be pretty overpowering and frightening.

Rising up out of depression is not only possible, it's what your Father wants for you as well. Remember, where joy is, God is. Where God abides, depression is nowhere to be found. But good feelings, the kind we're talking about that will help you build a pathway up to God, are also practically impossible to find from a place of depression. If you tell someone who's depressed to look on the bright side and try to find things to appreciate, they'll look at you as if you've lost your mind. In the dungeon of a mind that's experiencing depression, there is almost no light. I say almost no light for we are never really separate from God. There is always a thread there no matter how much we close down our connection. But you do feel as if God has shut off the power to your light.

When you're depressed, you have lost power to your light, but it's not Gods doing. We threw the switch. We may not even remember what led us to this closed-in feeling, but we don't have to. We don't have to retrace our steps to find the cause of our depression. So what to do? Believe it or not, the next rung up from depression is anger. When you're depressed, you can't breathe. You feel powerless. The lights are out. You need to feel heard, to lash out, to take revenge on the cause of your pain. "But wait a minute," you say, "isn't anger a bad feeling emotion? How can I climb the ladder back up to God if I'm moving toward anger? Won't that slam me with more of the same?" Well, you're half right. You will get slammed with more angry thoughts if you choose to stay in that angry place, guaranteed. And anger is a bad feeling emotion for most people, but it never is for someone who's depressed. For someone caught in depression, anger is a breath of fresh air. For someone who is depressed, anger and feelings of revenge feel much better than depression. And we can trust that God is in the direction of that better feeling if we keep going.

It could very well be that someone left you or wore you down in a harsh way. Or maybe you learned this place of depression from a parent or other important person in your life. When you reside in an atmosphere of separation from God, it's pretty normal to think that this is the normal state of things. It's no one's fault. The person who wronged you didn't know any better and probably learned it from someone else who didn't know any better.

It may be that to display anger to the person who hurt you will cause you more problems. Some people are more happy to have you be depressed, where you don't cause them any trouble. If you're angry, that's breaking the agreement with them and they may not like that. But the beauty of the marvelous mind that God gave us is that we don't have to engage it in the "real world" for it to have an affect on us. In other words, you can take a tennis racket into your room, and close the door and go at it on a pillow. Really give it to them. Tell them you're not going to take it anymore and whack your pillow good. Or you can yell at God. You can say, "Where were you? Aren't you supposed to be taking care of me? I'm so angry at you, I could scream!" Then scream for good measure. Don't worry, He can take it.

When my young daughter needs to let off some steam at me, I let her. I let her get as angry as she needs to get. For one reason or another she's temporarily cut herself off from God's current and she's caught, trapped in that place of despair. Sometimes a tantrum is the only way out. She can't articulate it, but she's so angry that she's cut off from God, because she knows at a deep level that life is supposed to feel better than this. And she's right. Usually it's something relatively insignificant that she's upset about, but the root cause is always feeling separated from God. When she yells at me, I just stay calm and mirror back to her the things she's yelling. "You're very upset, aren't you, that I wasn't able to fix your broken toy like you wanted. I can see that it's making you really angry that I didn't come through for you. I'd be angry too." After she's raged on for a while she usually comes and crawls into my lap and we comfort each other. Before you know it, we're both all smiles and laughter again. I can't help but think that God would treat us the same way.

But what about staying in anger? How does that feel good? Anger does not feel good for most people, but anger is in the direction of God for someone who is depressed. For someone who is just angry, they are way up the ladder towards better-feeling thoughts than someone who is depressed. But because anger is still a pretty self-destructive emotion, someone who is angry has to try to work themselves into something better-feeling than anger, like frustration. Look for ways to think of things in a slightly better way to work yourself back up the ladder.

It's a tough row to hoe when you're peeved, because you just want to be peeved. You're thinking, "Damn it! Why aren't things going my way? This stinks!" And for a while, that actually feels good. But because the object of your anger is not the cause of your pain, trying to force your problem to be different so you can feel better has no success at all. Your pain is always equal to your degree of separation from God. The source of your happiness is always God, so trying to get rid of your problem only compounds it because you are giving it so much attention. I never knew that trying to get rid of my problem by dwelling on it and trying to force it into a form that will be pleasing to me is simply impossible. We are like a fish on a hook and the more we struggle and push against our problem, the deeper the barb works its way in. The only way I'm going to feel better is when I turn in the direction of God and start walking. There really is one simple solution to every imaginable problem. It's connecting with God.

God Makes Goodness Easy

The Bible is filled with hard-to-follow rules, or at least that's the way it's always felt to me. For example, the rule about forgiveness. You mean I have to forgive that jerk at the office 70 x 7 times? Give me a break. They must not have had calculators back when they penned the Bible, because that's 490 times, and he's only used up 54. And how about this one: if someone asks me for my shirt, not only do I have to give it to them, he gets my jacket too? How is that fair? He should get a job and buy his own jacket! I know, often these rules are metaphorical and God gives us a lot of leeway in keeping them, but if I feel that I don't or can't measure up to God's rule-book, that guilt can have a poisonous effect on me. Feeling "not enough" not only doesn't feel good, if you keep it up long enough it will make you sick. I'm sure that wasn't the intent when this was all written down. I feel the same way about the over-emphasis on calling yourself and others sinners. As much as anything it's probably just a language issue that got twisted around by an enthusiastic preacher, gleefully condemning his flock for their wrong-doings. Sin has been accurately translated as missing the mark, but for many people the word sinner still conjures up images of hopeless deviants, lined up before of the gates of hell. I have to bring the conversation back to our loving Father analogy. My dear earthly father would have a hard time labeling his children sinners, in the sense of being bad or unworthy people. A loving God sees all of his children in the same way, each of them worthy, precious, and enough.

How do we keep up with all the rules to be good people without the rules themselves doing us in? Another quote helps us out: *The eye is the lamp of the body. If your eyes are good, your whole body will be full of light. But if your eyes are bad, your whole body will be full of darkness.* Here Jesus is talking about seeing the world differently, which leads us back to our key of looking for things to appreciate. If I spend my time looking for the best in people, reaching as far as I need to reach to find something good about every situation or person that tests my patience, I can gradually work myself into a state of joy. Now I'm on God's turf where everything is easy. When you're joyful, it's infinitely easier to love the people around you, no matter what kind of shenanigans they're engaged in. If you're feeling secure in that joyful place where God is always providing for you, it's easy to forfeit your shirt to that lazy guy but also to see him as not lazy. He's a child of God on his own personal journey to God. Why would you want to withhold your shirt from your child if he asked for it? You wouldn't, but because our eyes are clouded by feelings of lack, of not-enoughness, it seems hard to give up something to a stranger that we think we need and will be hard to replace.

Normally we expect the people around us to make us happy, but that's not their responsibility. If we spend the time to get in that happy place with God first, it removes our expectation that others behave in ways that please us. Then we're free - our happiness is not contingent on their cooperation, and this is so empowering. They can be who they are, flaws and all, and we can love them. They can even become the indirect cause of our happiness if our eyes get practiced at seeing others the way God sees them. When we look at someone with anything less than love, it feels bad, and not because they are bad, but because that viewpoint is so far from how God is looking at them. When we use our eyes to only see the negative aspects of each other, we veer away from God's presence. But when we use our eyes to see others the way God sees them, which is with unconditional love, we feel great. Unconditional - that means that the conditions don't have to change for God to love them. If I can get into that joyful place with Him, I won't need anyone to do anything differently in order for me to be blissfully with God. Then even 700 x 7 will be a piece of cake.

Your Unique Gift

Sometimes it seems like it would be a lot simpler if we all liked the same things, and if we all agreed that there was one best way to do something. God apparently had other plans. If you look at nature, diversity rules. There is not just one kind of plant, there are millions of kinds of plants. The same goes for animals, bugs, fish, birds, bacteria, and luckily, people. But we humans are chronic pigeon-holers. We love to categorize and divide the world up into little neat boxes. I'm white, you're black. I'm American, you're Chinese. I'm old, you're young. Maybe it makes us feel better if we can identify and label the things we bump into in life so we know where we fit in.

People are as unique as it gets. There is only one me, and one you. The things I like are unique to me and the things that you like are unique to you. Fortunately, this is the way God created us. My wife loves to go to parties, I find big groups uncomfortable. I love to perform on a stage, my wife would find a spinal tap more pleasant. We enjoy a number of things together, but we also enjoy different things.

In the same way, each of us is endowed with unique gifts. Everyone has a unique talent or skill or just something that they enjoy doing a lot. I've always loved the movie *Chariots of Fire*. The rising track star in the film spoke about how God made him fast and when he was running, he felt God's pleasure. That young athlete had found his calling, the thing he loved to do. And the clue he's giving us is this: when he engaged in his passion, he felt God's pleasure. This is really great news. By doing the thing that I love, I am automatically growing closer to God, and the even better news is this: The thing that I love to do, which is also the thing that brings me closer to God, also happens to be my unique gift from God that I have to give to the world. Isn't that grand?

I used to think that to be a good person, I had to select from a list of *Approved Services to Humanity* and perform some duty from that list whether I liked it or not. But serving others is much, much better than that. God gave me something I'm good at and that I enjoy, and I get to revel in it, explore it, be it. When I share this thing with others, it fulfills a precise need in them. It's a perfect arrangement, all orchestrated by the Master Conductor.

Children know how to do this well, and it's called playing. They don't play to accomplish anything, or to get anywhere. They absorb themselves in play because it's fun to align with God. When my 7 year old daughter is absorbed in her playing, and she's singing while joyfully preparing a bed for her baby dolls, it brings me such happiness to watch her. That's her unique gift to me. She's not playing to make me happy, she's playing in the eternal now with God because it is joyful for her to do that. I can't think that our Father would feel any different about us when we get absorbed in our play, in our passion.

What about the people who like to bomb, or kill or otherwise hurt others? Is God pleased with them? It's true that there are people who are engaged in activities that hurt other people, but no one who is connected to God would ever hurt another living being. Those people are so disconnected from who they really are, which is a worthy, loved child of God, that they can't tell the difference between what feels good and what feels bad. They are so pinched off from God's love that they are the walking wounded, so used to feeling bad that it feels normal. Not to worry though, God hasn't given up on them and never will. One day, they too will learn how to play. Do you know how to play?

The Garden Wall

I've found that a very difficult tendency to uproot in myself is that of finding comfort in criticism. I still don't grasp why it is that we do it. Some say there is a certain security in thinking we are better than someone else, but I don't know if that's the whole story. We just got it backwards at some point. Children do not have that critical tendency to find fault with the world and the people in it. I remember being astonished when our daughter first started to talk and she described how she saw the world. Young children literally see no evil - they see only God. Everything is just fine to them, everyone is beautiful. They do not see black people and white people - they see only people. They see everyone with the eyes of God, but as children get older I think we adults just squeeze it out of them and the flawed thinking is passed to the next generation. When children grow up and leave childhood, it reminds me of Adam and Eve, and being in the Garden, then suddenly finding yourself outside the Garden wall and unable to even see back in.

Whatever the reason for the fall, here we are. The challenge now is to get back in the Garden. People love to be around young children because children are a window into God's realm. They have still not lost that ecstatic abandon of being in constant play on God's playground. You can sometimes shoplift a little time with God by playing with a child, but if you can't maintain that connection to Him, you can't stay there. I think that's why we want to lash out at others with our criticism. I'm having a tantrum, clamoring to get back in the Garden, and I'm blaming all the other people and objects and situations in my world for it. I think they are the ones keeping me out of the Garden. I know in my heart that the Garden exists - that place of peace, joyful creativity, abundance and non-judgment, where we play endlessly with God. I want to be there more than anything in the world. But because the world we experience is so in our face, and actual pain seems to be emanating from these people and situations in our lives, it's a natural instinct to want to protect ourselves and defensively lash out. The world is painful so it must be the world that I have to change if I want to extinguish my pain.

These words rocked my world when I first heard them: *The people, things and conditions in your world are not the cause of your pain. Your separation from God is the only cause of pain.* It made perfect sense. I couldn't put it into practice immediately, but I understood it, and that one concept has had such practical and profound consequences in helping me go towards the place where God is. The real and only protection from the painful things in life is God. But it's not as if God is going to swoop down and smite all the bad guys with a big hurricane and purify the world of all those people you don't like. I always found the biblical examples to be confusing on this point. God does do a lot of swooping down and smiting the bad guys in the Bible, but I could never believe in anything but a loving God so there was this big contradiction. The answer to that paradox is this: God does get rid of our enemies, but He does it on an individual level within our hearts once you re-learn to be in the Garden again. Those who warn that God is going to cast death and destruction upon the wicked aren't telling us what God would do, they're telling us what they would do if they were God!

God makes it so easy. He saves me the trouble of

having to run myself ragged trying to rid the world of rascals. The day I begin looking for where God is manifesting in all the people and situations in my life, all those rascals will start to high-tail it out of town. Because in doing that, I am moving closer to the Garden. I am leaning in the direction of joy when I look for positive aspects, and God is always in the direction of joy.

Giving extra special attention to someone's perceived flaws is probably the worst thing I can do to myself, and it doesn't help them any, either. I live in a world of trouble when that's my tendency. And the worst part is that I'm giving extra attention to things I do not want. Focusing on the world's perceived flaws crowds out God and keeps that broken record skipping. I want to listen to a different record, the song of the Garden.

Perception

There are two distinct ways of perceiving the world that contradict each other in an interesting way. On one hand we have what we'll call the objective world, that we all agree is composed of solid objects like cars, rocks, water, people and so forth. But when we start to look at that "objective" world, our mind invisibly adds something to the mix that make the objects seem anything but solid. Two people can look at the same thing and see it in completely opposite ways. Then we get into big arguments about which interpretation is correct. For instance, we can probably each say, with a serious face, that we believe that the candidate we supported for the last presidential campaign was the best one, or at least less bad than their opponent. And we may have also said that there was no way we could be wrong about that. Did you ever think about the impossibility of this situation? Our solid, objective world just became very wobbly. Once we start interacting with something in our world and believing that it has the power to make us happy or unhappy, the way we look at it changes. When it appears to benefit us we see it as a good thing, and when it appears to curtail our happiness in some way we see it as not so good.

This in turn leads us to believe that in order to create happiness, we need to change how the world and other people behave. So most of us go to work at a very early age, trying to get the world to conform to our perfect picture of the way we think the world should be. If I could just get my boss to not do that thing that's driving me crazy. If I could just get my government to not tax me so much. If I could just figure out how to get people to stop polluting the earth. If I could just get my kids to study harder. And we can spend a lifetime trying to erase all the badness we see. But that really is going about it the hard way. Haven't you noticed?

Here's where we really have to let go of this death-grip we've got on life and trying to make it conform to what we think is a perfect world. As long as everybody has their own idea of what would constitute a perfect world, we are never, ever going to agree on what that is. If we are never going to agree, we are never going to be happy. If you think that the people in your life have to behave in the way you think is best before you can be happy, then I hope you look good in orange. Welcome to Alcatraz.

Not to worry, though. You know how you're going to escape from Alcatraz. You're going to ask the Big Man. His escape plan is foolproof, easy and it won't cost you a dime. You just have to make connecting with Him the most important thing in the world to you. There is nothing that even comes close in importance. Because once you connect with Him, he takes on every single problem that is troubling you, and then the world doesn't need fixing anymore. Maybe you can't even begin to imagine the solutions to the problems you see out there. Luckily, you don't have to. That's God's work. Your only work is to be with God.

You will never clean up the world of all the wrongs you see in it, but you can start to try to see the world as God sees it. You may be wondering what makes me so special that I know how God sees the world? Simple. When I feel love coursing through me when I look at another, when I see the world with the eyes of a child, in fascination with its complexity and beauty, when I laugh about things that used to be a sharp pain in my heart, I can only conclude that this is God's love, beauty and joy I'm experiencing, for love, beauty and joy do not exist separate from Him. Everyone is going to have to come to their own conclusions about whether or not they are connected to God. No person or rule or book or anything outside of you is ever going to be able to make that determination. You're the only one who will be able to tell if God is talking to you. For me, the level of joy I feel, or not, is the acid test. When I feel joy, it's easy for me to love others, to be a good person, to be generous, to put others first, to do all the things God asks us to do. I can't help but think that this is God, working through me, for apart from God, there is no joy.

In my opinion, the main purpose of the Bible is to show you how to connect with God. If you haven't connected with God in a deep way, your interpretation of the Bible may not be at fault, but your lack of willingness to apply it to yourself may be. I spent a lot of my life worrying about which interpretation of scripture was the correct one, and trying to convince others that my interpretation was the correct one without ever actually using my interpretation to go to God. It wasn't a waste of time - I don't think God sees it like that. All the time and skinned knees a child expends in learning to walk is never a waste. But now I know that if I'm angry, upset, worried or in despair about my life, I can be pretty sure that I'm not listening to what God has to say to me, because if I am in a close communion with God, those emotions won't be a part of my makeup. I may dip into them on occasion, but I always know how to reverse the trend and get back into alignment with Him. Then once again I'll be seeing the world through God's eyes. The day I can consistently begin to find things to appreciate about the situations and people in my life, that's the day I can begin to see God's world. It's a sweet place to live.

Careers

Earlier, we talked about your unique gift. Something that you love to do, or are really good at. God planted that gift in you, and the reason it thrills you to engage in it is because that's God talking to you. That thrilling, joyful feeling is God's pleasure being felt by you. But as long as you don't go towards the gift God planted in you, you'll feel frustrated and cheated by life.

For instance, if what you really love to do more than anything is garden, you just have to start listening to that call if you want to be fulfilled. If when you garden you feel connected to your true self and to God, I'd pay special attention to that feeling. That's God saying, "Come to me, beloved child, I'm here in this place where you find joy. Come to me, dwell with me, where I'll provide you with everything you want." It isn't being selfish to go towards the thing that you love, because that's just you being drawn to where God is for you. There's that funny idea coming in again - that doing God's will has to be an unpleasant, selfless task to accomplish or test that we have to pass before He'll hand over the goodies.

God is in different places for everyone on the planet. If you're a dedicated surgeon, He's in that zone of intense focus and precision when you're repairing someone's body. If you're a dancer, He's in that place of physical ease and ecstatic movement. If you're a teacher, He's in that thrill of helping a child learn a new skill that makes them more able. It's different for everyone. God has planted a seed in each of us, and finding that seed, and watering it and nurturing it will draw us closer to

God's will for us. God has His attention only on what is good for us and feels good to us.

I grew up under the impression that making money and doing what you love have to be two different things, and it's a belief that dies hard. Making money meant that you very likely had to do something unpleasant, and doing something that you loved was something you did in your spare time. If you've spent a lifetime ignoring that call from God, it's naturally going to be hard to start listening to what He wants for you. When we ignore God's call, we try to make up for the lack of abundance He would deliver through our gift by doing things to make money that we don't really want to do. We think, "Well, God isn't going to come through for me, so let me make up for this lack of resources by taking it into my own hands, even though I don't like this job I've found."

It's helpful to always go back to our Good Father analogy. If you were the father in control of the purse-strings, would you make your child do something unpleasant to earn their allowance? Or would you encourage them to make beautiful music, beautiful art, build beautiful tree houses and other things your child enjoys, and reward them for that? God's way will always be the way of ease, of enjoyment, of playing in the eternal now of His presence.

"I get that I love gardening more than my dead-end job. But how can I make a living gardening? I hate having to go to my cubicle at work and sit at a computer all day. TGIF when I can finally go home and do what I really love."

First of all, getting out of your dead-end job will never happen by hating that job and living for Fridays - in fact that's a good way to make sure you stay stuck in that job, because that's where you're putting your attention. Giving something your attention, even negative attention, will cause that thing to grow. So how can we make the switch to using God's gift as our conduit to money, instead of our life-sucking 9 to 5 job? We use our key, of course. We enter into a close communion with God by looking for things in His marvelous creation that we enjoy, no matter how small. You can find those things everywhere if you try. Start looking at your job for things to appreciate, even if the only good thing you can say about your job is that your chair is comfortable. You have to reach as far as you can reach sometimes to start seeing the world through God's eyes, where everything is a source of joy. Once you grab on to that tiny goodness, and then another and another, soon you'll be moving into God's vicinity and it will get easier and easier. He'll start opening doors for you, doors that were there all along but that you couldn't even see. He'll start introducing you to new people and projects at work that pique your interest and open other doors. You'll start meeting other gardeners, maybe even at work, who want to explore your shared interest together. Keep the ball rolling and in a very short time you may find it possible to cut back on your day job one day a week because you've found a part-time job consulting for a landscaper. *Keep the focus on what you want to see in your life, not on what you don't want to see.* Going towards joy is always going towards God. Where God is, there you'll find unlimited opportunity and resources. We can play in God's house whenever we make the decision that God is what we want and start going towards His joy. His house all around us if we get good at seeing it.

Running Away From Problems

Once you're in a secure place with God, you'll no longer have to run from your problems - they will run from you instead. Often when we bump up against a painful or frustrating situation, we make a vow to do things differently so that the pain can't hit us again. Let's say you're with someone and they aren't treating you right. So you leave that person and it feels better for a while, then you hook up with someone else and find that the new one isn't treating you so well either. Or maybe you're not being appreciated at work or being given the plum assignments. So you decide you'll find another job where they'll treat you better, but when you go to a new job it seems that you've taken the old job with you.

The problem is not that you're not being treated right by your spouse, or that they're not appreciating you at work. It may very well be that your spouse is doing things that you don't like, and that the people at work are taking actions that are painful to you. But you have to get used to the idea that the real pain in your heart isn't emanating from those people and situations, so running from them or trying to change them in some way has no effect on your situation. The real pain is that you are temporarily separating yourself from God.

Keep reminding yourself, when the pain comes, that this is God calling you home. God loves His children without exception and stands willing and ready to help you find a remedy to your problem. But if you keep thinking that you can fix your problems by doing this or that, you actually perpetuate it by keeping your attention there instead of on God. By affixing your attention to the problem, you keep it alive and kicking. The trick is to take your attention off the problem and put it on the solution that God has already prepared for you.

When you're where God is, always remember that it feels good in your heart, so the only action you need to take when the problem rears its ugly head is to do whatever you can to feel a little bit better. Maybe you can't find anything to appreciate about your spouse or your job. When you're in the thick of it, and God seems nowhere near, it's hard to see things a new way. If this is the case, you can switch your attention to anything else that does feel better when you look at it. Being with a child or a pet might do it for you, or going to an engrossing movie. Just take a small action that takes the charge off of the thing that's got you upset. Sometimes that's all it takes to get moving in the direction of God. Once you're feeling a little better about things, maybe then you can start finding something to appreciate about your spouse or job. It's important to note that you're not trying to find something about them to appreciate so they'll change. The only reason to look for things to appreciate is because this connects you with God again. Then whether they change or not is of no consequence because you're happily in God's Garden.

You only have to move up one rung at a time, so

every step you take, no matter how small, takes you a little further in His direction. As you move closer to the way He sees His world, it gets easier and easier. Eventually, when you get even the slightest into God's vicinity, your problem will just crumble. You won't even be able to remember why it was that you were upset. In every person, object or situation, there will be things that you like and things you don't like. It's up to you to choose to look at the things that you like. God stands in that place, where He doesn't see anyone's faults. He only sees His child making their way home.

Rejoicing

One of the most enjoyable and powerful activities that we can experience is the act of rejoicing in God's blessings. It should be taught every week in every Sunday school. You can do it when you're just taking a walk or while you're in the midst of a busy task. The more you do it, the easier it gets, and the more its benefits grow. The positive results of rejoicing are tremendous and never-ending. The act of rejoicing can transform your world.

Rejoicing is a learned skill, or maybe I should say a forgotten skill, because we still knew how to do it when we were children. Before we squeeze it out of them, young children are perpetually in a state of rejoicing. They do it without thinking. The world is a magic place to them and they are constantly in awe of God's playground as they run from joy to joy. Everywhere they walk is holy ground, God is everywhere for them. They see only the goodness in life. They aren't afraid of tomorrow because there is literally no tomorrow for children. The concept of time is not something they have the least interest in. They trust that everything is being provided for them, and they are correct to reside in that trust, in the lap of God. They are much wiser than we are on that count. We force our children to care about time because we do. We have things to do and places to go. We think that there is something that we have to finish in life. My daughter is seven now and she is blissfully still not cursed by an awareness of time. It's hard not to force time on our children, isn't it?

"But children don't have to worry about tomorrow. They don't have to pay the bills, go to work, meet the budgets."

What's wrong with that argument is that we can still do all those things and never worry about tomorrow if we can get back into the Garden with God. One of the keys to the Garden is rejoicing in God's blessings. The only thing crucial to accomplish in life is to get back into the Garden, where God is. The Garden is the place that we've fooled ourselves into thinking is to be found in achievements, people, family, and possessions, so we run after those things and exhaust ourselves in the process and then get angry when they don't measure up. We make it so hard, and God wants to make it easy for us.

If we can re-learn to rejoice, we're home free. There is nothing to accomplish in the Garden but being with God and listening to His guidance. Then we'll find that all the perfect careers, people, family, and possessions we've ever wanted have always been in the Garden but we couldn't see them. We've got it completely flipped around. God has already given us everything we need but because our focus is on what we don't have, we can't see it and we feel cheated by life.

Worse than cancer or crime or pollution is constantly thinking we don't have enough and comparing ourselves to others. Cancer can only kill you, but comparing yourself to others can put you directly in hell, today. When we see someone with a more successful career, or anything we perceive to be something that we want, it drives us crazy. The worst part is that we lose what God has already blessed us with by thinking about what we don't have. It's not enough that we compare ourselves to things in the present. We project a virtual copy of ourselves into the future and use that as an excuse to ruin our lives today. We worry about not having enough money in the future, or good health or a clean planet or any number of things. It is a useful skill to some degree to be able to envision future events, but when we start being unhappy that the dream we have about the future isn't here yet, or worry that the future won't be what we want it to be, all that envisioning no longer serves us.

It's not that you're breaking God's Commandment if you covet and you'll go to hell when you die. It's that you send yourself to hell in that moment - no need to die first. Because compared to being in the Garden, wanting something you think you can't have is hell because it separates you from God.

With God, we can have the things we want in life. What do you want in life? I want to feel exhilaration and passion. I want to love everyone. I want to create amazing things with my life. I want to give the world the very best that I have. I want to feel chills up my spine because I feel God near. I want to live joyfully and fully. When I fall into bed at night, I want to be exhausted that I ran full out, loving, playing, creating, growing. In other words, I want to be with God in his playground again. All those things are in the Garden.

If I care about being with God, then caring about rejoicing has to be my number one priority. When negative emotion pops up, this is my cue to do an about-face because I can always be certain that God is *never* in the direction of any negative emotion. In the moment I realize that I'm becoming angry or jealous, if I can tear my attention away from whatever has got my goat and put it onto some blessing that God is showering me with, I can close the door to hell. Rejoicing turns the flames of hell into a soothing, cool stream.

Sometimes it pains me when my daughter says she wants to be older because I don't want her to be cursed by the things adults do to themselves. But it doesn't have to be that way. Rejoicing cures all this. Once we get into a good habit of rejoicing in the infinite blessings God is bestowing on us, the goodness that we are experiencing is magnified exponentially. In the Garden, God gives us all we need and all the answers to our questions. Our life has meaning and richness, and what may or may not come in the future doesn't haunt us anymore.

The Magic Chapter

When *people* don't behave like we want them to, we become miserable. Then we complicate it by praying to God that those *people* change. And sometimes when we do this, the *people* actually become worse. We can even start thinking that God is testing us or punishing us, which is something He never does. The problem with praying that God change *people* is that we mistakenly think we know what would fix them. It's crystal clear to us that if those *people* would just start shaping up, everything would iron itself out. But that is basing our happiness on what *people* do or don't do. A little risky. Maybe more than a little. We need to replace our attention on *people* with attention to God. Once we reach the Garden and turn it over to Him, He removes the suffering from every aspect of our lives. Once we make it even a little close to the Garden, it seems like God starts changing the *people* in our world to suit us. But what is actually happening is that we are seeing with God's eyes, and God's world is perfect just like it is because God can't separate Himself from perfection.

What's magic about this chapter is that you can replace the word *people* in the paragraph above with anything you're having trouble with and get the solution. God is the one fix for every problem we could ever dream of. Below are some replacement words to try out. Feel free to add some of your own.

Governments, Politicians, Children, Supervisors, Parents, Relatives, Teachers, Students, Clients,

Customers, Peaceniks, War Mongers, Republicans, Democrats, Congregations, Muslims, Catholics, Protestants, Homosexuals, Heterosexuals, Men, Women.

You don't ever have to figure out any of your problems anymore. You don't need to analyze your problems, spend hours on the phone trying to sort them out, drive all over creation to fix them, explain your problems to others so they can help you figure them out. As much as I wanted to believe that it was, I learned that the solution to my problem is in no way associated with the problem. I used to think that the harder I pushed against my problem, the faster the solution would arrive. This misconception confused me for decades. I kept thinking, if there is some way I can solve this then I'm good. If I can get this person to not do this one thing that is driving me nuts, then I'll be happy. If I can just figure how to pay all these bills, then we're golden. If I can just figure out which treatment or therapist or support group is the right one, then my problems are over. The error in this is thinking that the solution to your problem is in the same sphere as the problem, but it isn't. This is because every solution you need comes from God, and where God is there are no problems. If you put being with God first, He makes your world perfect, and you don't have to lift a finger.

If you leave your life exactly as it is right now but simply start intentionally appreciating all of God's blessings He is bestowing on you, He will begin to take over for you. There has to be nothing more important to you than that, because once you begin to consistently get into that way of thinking, all the problems you have are solved. All the confusion about what to do is cleared up. All your fears about what may happen in the future are ended. There really is nothing more to it than that.

⚷ Prayer

What is prayer if we break it down to its basic purpose? Isn't it an attempt to commune with God? Then communing with God is getting myself to that place where I really feel joyful. He is there, in that place, wherever that is for you.

But you might say, "How can God be in that place, and I be with God, if my grandmother is dying of some debilitating illness? How can I possibly feel good in those circumstances?" God gives us a choice about this, always. You can be with Him, where it's joyful, or you can focus on something that separates you from Him, like your grandmother's illness. "But isn't that abandoning my grandmother?" God never said you have to abandon anyone. The only thing you have to do is commit to putting Him above all other things with all your heart, soul and mind. In this case it means focusing only on the aspects of your grandmother that you are happy about because that's all God cares about. If you really want to help her, that is the most beneficial thing you can do. It's powerful prayer to focus on the essence of how God sees her.

Prayer is thinking about all the things you love about her, remembering all the great times you've shared with her, thinking about memories of her when she was vital and healthy. If she was a great cook, milk it. If she was good at shuffling cards, milk that. If she was good at comforting you when you were a little boy, really milk that too. If she made a killer country-style steak, milk that. There is nothing too small when it comes to rejoicing. Because once you climb up a few rungs by thinking about these aspects of her, more of these happy thoughts about her will occur to you and you'll fly up a few more rungs, where you'll start to receive inspiration from God. When you align with God, the path lights up, and confusion drops away. Then you'll really be able to help your grandmother. You'll know what she needs and what will help her the most, because God is showing you. In addition, God will lead you to all the people, situations and resources that will help you to help your grandmother. God acts as a magnifying glass, increasing your ability to see the solution He's already prepared for you. Talk about a reason to love God!

Loving yourself

I've found that loving yourself is essential, if you want to be with God. Jesus talked a lot about how you should give up everything to be with God, even yourself. Give up your family, your life, your possessions. I was confused for a while about this because Jesus did say those things, but a harsh interpretation of his words crept in somehow and left me with the idea that it's hard work and a sacrifice to be with God, as if the only way to get to Him was through painful struggle. I thought that way for a long time, and I can tell you from experience, it's not helpful at all. Getting to Him through an unpleasant struggle is literally impossible. You can see how the example in the Bible could be confusing, because you may want to work hard at connecting to God, in the sense that you want to spend as much time doing it as you can. And it is a struggle in that you're struggling to remind yourself constantly that your only work is to find things to be joyful about. But a hard struggle, in the sense of unpleasant, is never a part of the journey. God is simply not where anything unpleasant is.

When Jesus said we need to sell everything and give the money to the poor and leave our family to be with Him, I believe He meant that we should put God first, and metaphorically have that garage sale and leave our family. When we put being with God first, we are not held hostage by our possessions or other people or our family by expecting them to make us happy - we "leave" them and seek our happiness in God.

When you don't love yourself, the reason it feels bad is because God does love you and that thought of not loving yourself is so very far from how He thinks about you. God has a crush on you. You are so adorable and lovable in His eyes. You are perfect just as you are, you don't need to change in the slightest for God to have unbounded love for you. When we think otherwise, we separate ourselves from God. When we don't like ourselves, or think we're stupid, or bad, or should be doing better, we are disagreeing with how God feels about us. We are saying to Him, "I know you have omniscient awareness of everything in the universe, but on this one, Big Man, you've got it wrong."

We're the ones who have it all wrong, and we can tell by the way we feel. It feels bad when we criticize ourselves. It feels good when we pat ourselves on the back for doing a good job at something. The reason it feels good is because that's what God is doing. If God didn't feel that way about us, that joy would not even exist for us to feel, because there is no joy separate from God!

It feels good when we pamper ourselves a little bit, indulge ourselves with some personal time once in a while, because God is happy when we enjoy our life.

I once went to a Fathers Conference where there were all kinds of workshops and seminars about how to be a better dad. My favorite workshop was the one where the facilitator told us, "I'm not worried that you're not good fathers. You wouldn't be at this conference if you weren't pretty good dads already. But what I want to try to get you to do is be a little more selfish, because when you take better care of yourself, you'll have more to give." He went on to encourage all the dads in the room to work at carving out some "me time" once in a while to feed ourselves. He told us to exercise, go to a movie, read a book, take a long bath, pamper ourselves a little more. Then we'll be re-charged and will become even better at fathering. This was great for all us over-committed dads to hear. Moms would do well to adopt this, too. In fact everyone should. Just like the dads at the conference, if you're interested in having a relationship with God, it's a given that you are a good person, and you're trying. So give yourself a break and love yourself a little more. Loving yourself will help give you the energy to keep going towards your goal of being with God.

When you are looking for things to appreciate, don't forget to include yourself in that list. God apparently had something special in mind when He created you, and you need to acknowledge that. Regularly pat yourself on the back for a job well done. Shine a light on your good qualities and ignore the parts you don't like. If you do this, your good qualities will magnify and become even better. Keep it up and I guarantee you that your good qualities will eventually crowd out the things you don't like about yourself.

If you're not enjoying life, having fun with everyone, laughing a lot, singing in the shower and so forth, you might want to add loving yourself to your toolbox. It will help you get to God quicker.

Getting Stuff

Here's a really interesting quote from Jesus: *I tell you the truth, if anyone says to this mountain, 'Go, throw yourself into the sea,' and does not doubt in his heart but believes that what he says will happen, it will be done for him. Therefore I tell you, whatever you ask for in prayer, believe that you have received it, and it will be yours.* So, according to Jesus, you can ask God for anything and he'll deliver.

"Really? COOL! I want a Prius! And a Playstation. And Guitar Hero and a 3G iPhone. And abs of steel while you're at it." Okay, God will give you all those things, but first you gotta LTLYGWAYHAWAYSAWAYM! It doesn't make for a very elegant acronym, does it? OK, I'll spell it out: *Love the Lord your God with all your heart and with all your soul and with all your mind.* How do you do that? Get happy. How do you do that? Look for things in God's awesome creation to appreciate and rejoice about. Keeping your attention on those things multiplies your happiness and you become really joyful. Then you're in with God and He turns over the booty. Done.

But along the way you may discover that once you get happy, the thing that you wanted because you thought it would make you happy transforms into something else. That's just God giving you something even better than what you were asking for in the first place. Like a BMW hybrid instead of a Prius. Just kidding. But once you get into a close communion with God, He automatically knows what you want and is flowing it to you, much better than you can imagine it.

For practically my whole life, I've done a funny thing. When I see something I want, whether it is a thing, or a relationship, or a state of mind, or an achievement of any kind, I believe that I'll succeed if I just mimic the actions of others who have succeeded before me. Seems like the logical thing to do, doesn't it? You see someone put a seed into the ground, and water it and they get a result, so you follow what they do and expect the same result. But have you noticed how the method of doing what others have done, even when followed to a T, can have a hit-or-miss quality to it? The fruit is not always forthcoming. It can make life seem like a treadmill when you're hammering away at a project, or a relationship, or state of body or mind that you're hoping will bear fruit, when the ultimate outcome seems so out of your control.

In one way of looking at it, it's true that we have no control whatsoever over the outcome of our actions. What happens to me today I have almost no control over. However, when you add God into the equation, we have ultimate control. God will guarantee a perfect outcome in all our endeavors, in whatever area of life you desire an improvement in. But you have to let Him in first. I say let in, because it's an opening up, a releasing yourself into His Garden that enables it all to happen.

An incredibly easy and effective method for allowing this releasing to happen is rejoicing.

So much of our energy is spent on forcing the things around us to conform to what we want, but if we could release the responsibility to God, He would do all the work. We only have one task, and completing this one task will create such an easy, happy life for us. Aligning with God is all we have to do. Go to bed rejoicing, wake up rejoicing. Find the things in life that give you joy, and give them your full attention. These are God's gifts to you, His personal blessings to you. Getting into the mood of rejoicing about those blessings is great fun. It's reason to celebrate when you're getting back into the Garden. Once you give up all the hard work, it frees up huge amounts of your energy. Then, when God inspires you to act, you're ready to spring into action with everything you've got. How odd that for all those years, I couldn't see God's wonderful gifts, all around me. Recognizing them is the only thing standing between me and the Garden.

Reaching the various goals we have in our life involves fostering a belief that we've already received what we're asking for, which I believe we have. One of the best ways to incubate that kind of belief is to get into that joyful place with God first, then think about the thing you want as if you already have it. Think about how it will feel, think about why you want it, get into a really fun and appreciative place, imagining yourself experiencing it, and be hopeful and expectant about your success. Don't waste a second thinking about how it's going to come - those are minor details that God will take care of.

But here's the tricky part: you're not doing this to get the thing you're asking God for, but to get even further into that joyful, close communion with God. That place of joy is where all your stuff is. Keep doing this, then sit back and enjoy the journey, and the perfect essence of the thing you ask God for will eventually come, whether it's a state of being, an object or a situation. A funny thing though - when our prayer is answered, the details are always better than we imagined them, because our Father is looking after us.

What would happen if everyone got what they wanted? Decadence? Debauchery? I wouldn't worry about that, God put several safety features in place. First of all, if you are in alignment with God, it's impossible for you to ask for something inappropriate. And if you're not in alignment with God, getting what you really want in life is next to impossible - haven't you noticed? If I go around thinking that I'm less-than, insignificant and unworthy, my life will naturally reflect that. Conversely, someone who is connected to God is a thousand times more wise, influential, capable and loving than someone who is not. If everyone truly got connected with God and were letting His bounty in, it would be wonderful world.

But, what if I'm married to someone and I want something and my spouse wants something completely different? Again, not to worry. This is God we're talking about, the "with God nothing is impossible" guy, remember? So just line up with Him, focus only on what you want and let your spouse focus on what they want, and God will find a way to give you both the essence of what you each want. You think God can't do that? You have to understand that getting to God is the ultimate short cut. All we have to do is get to Him and everything we could possibly want comes as part of the package.

So if all you have to do to have a joyful, miraculous life is be in a constant state of appreciating your life and loving God, that's a pretty good deal. And if in your heart you still really, really want that 3G iPhone, no problem. That's peanuts to the Big Man.

God so wants His children to be happy that He's ready and willing to bend over backwards to do it. It doesn't seem this way sometimes because we are so practiced at instinctively reacting to our environment instead of keeping our focus on God. When things don't go our way we push against whatever is happening, and that pushing ends up magnifying the very thing we're trying to get rid of. It's a seductive trap because we really believe that if we can just push hard enough in exactly the right way, we can force our situation to change. It's easy to see why we stay stuck in situations that we don't like and deduce from this that God is either absent or ignoring our plight. God is always right there, holding the things we want in his hand like the good Father He is, ready to give it to us, but we are so stuck on focusing on the bad thing we are trying to get rid of that we take our focus off God.

God is where everything we want is. Everything. When we are pushing against the things we don't want in our world, whether it's a person, a situation, a physical condition, an object, a law, anything at all, we can tell that we are moving in the opposite direction from God because it feels bad when we do it. If the pushing felt good, we could be sure that we are moving toward God, but it never feels good. You would think we would learn after a while, but the dynamics of how it all works is hidden from us. Like Adam and Eve outside the Garden wall, we've eaten from the Tree of Knowledge and the way we view the world conspires against us to keep paradise hidden. We've divided the world up into good and evil and believe that we have power over which of those triumph. We mistakenly think we are the ones who hold the power to change things.

So how do we line up with God? How do we gain entry back into the Garden where we can partake of all the things that God has readied for us? The only power I have is the power in this very moment to decide if I want to go towards God or away from God. That's it. But fortunately, that's enough. Because if I choose to go towards God, He steps forward and gives me the key to the Garden gate.

Once again we return to our method. God is always in the direction of joy, so when we go towards joy, we go towards God. It's so easy and effortless once you get the hang of it. Getting started can be a little rocky, but if you keep at it, getting to God is child's play. Just make it your top priority to go through your day looking for things to appreciate about God's magnificent world. Say to yourself when you start your day, "Today I will be joyful, and rejoice in God's blessings wherever I can find them. I will scour my world for things to appreciate. I will choose to look only for those things which bring me joy."

"How can I look for good things when this bad thing has got my attention? It's horrible, the things those people are doing."

They may indeed be doing a horrible thing, but if I choose to look at it instead of moving in the direction of God, I can't blame them for that. It's my doing. Once you start looking for things to appreciate consistently, life becomes so sweet, because you are walking into the Garden. Everywhere you look, you see God's perfection, His magnificence. You not only start to be happier, you start to feel better, too. Once you start to feel better, you start to see everything in a whole new light because you're not expecting the world to change to make you happy. Your happiness is coming from God now. You start letting Him take the reins and take on changing all those rascals. He can handle them much better than you can, anyway. When you start to get into the Garden, magically, the people and situations in your immediate world will start to become sources of happiness instead of sources of frustration. The very same people who before had driven you out of your mind change before your eyes into the beautiful children of God that they've been all along, all of them on their own personal journeys to Him. What a relief!

🔑 Helping Others

Human relationships make up the bulk of our experience here on earth. There are so many different people in our lives, and each of them require our time and energy. We want to do the right thing in all our relationships, but sometimes it's hard to know what to do in each situation. For instance, I want to help my daughter to grow up to be happy and fulfilled, but exactly what is the best way to do that? Likewise, I want to be a good husband and friend to my wife, and I want her to be happy as well. Then there are the people at work. They all have different expectations of me and compete for my time. I want to help them with what they need and balance that with my own desire for a rich and fulfilling experience at work. Then we have dozens of satellite relationships with our community and world that we want to honor. When you add it up, that's a lot of pressure, all these people wanting things from you, and you wanting to be as good as you can be for them.

Fortunately, we don't have to figure out the best way of helping each of these people. God has done all the heavy lifting for us. If I want to be the best father I can possibly be for my daughter, to guide her in the perfect way to a rich and fulfilling life, there is only one thing I need to do. If I connect with God's love and get lined up with His will for me, he will show me exactly the most perfect, efficient and effective way to give my daughter what she needs. And in each of my other relationships, the same dynamic applies.

My primary responsibility to others is to align with God. It's not to fix them, or to train them or to correct them, thank God, for how could I ever figure out that? There are too many of them and they're all different and need different things. If I first take the time to align with God, all my relationships become effortless. If I don't take that time to connect to God, I literally wander through life in a hit or miss fashion, sometimes having success, sometimes not. If I line up with God, I'll have clarity about what to do because He's showing me. I'll have the wisdom to say the right thing, because I'm operating from a connection to His wisdom. The most important thing that my connection to God does for others is that they can witness me first hand, living a life of ease and happiness with God at the helm. They'll see me moving through the world and confronting problems at the same moment that God produces the solution. They'll see what I do to re-align with God when I fall away from time to time. They'll see the process of that constant course-correction to seek closeness to Him. Once they witness my living relationship with God and how it provides everything I could possibly want in life, they'll see how to give that to themselves as well. And that is the most precious gift you could ever give anyone.

Playing In The Sandbox

Children offer us another insight into God's Garden. When children are lost in play, they aren't concerned with how correct another child's play seems to them.

It sounds strange to even put it in those terms because that idea is so foreign to who children are. Two children can be side by side in the sandbox, and be totally happy and engrossed in the play they are each creating. Neither of them will look at the way the other is playing and say, "He's not really playing right. It's really upsetting me that he isn't playing right. I think I better show him how it's done." In the moment of play, each child is in the lap of God, not a care in the world, and could not be any happier. They are at the center of their universe, which is exactly where God is for them. It doesn't mean beans to them how effective or not another child's playing is.

I, on the other hand, am really excellent at determining whether or not someone else's life is being played correctly. It's so completely obvious to me how someone else should be behaving, for I can see with my own eyes how they are living. But when I say this to you, I deny your connection to God.

Everything with consciousness is deeply connected with God whether we can see it or not. God is talking to each of us all day, every day. When I think that you are not properly connected to God, I am in that very moment disconnecting myself from God. God will never say that you are not living your life correctly because He sees no faults in anyone. His eyes are incapable of seeing imperfection, because He can't separate Himself from perfection. Remember the clue God always gives us - if it feels bad in my heart, I'm moving away from His guidance. If it feels good, I'm moving toward Him. If I'm thinking my brother is playing life wrong, or is somehow less than me, there's no way that can feel good.

It may seem like God isn't taking care of things because people seem to be misbehaving left and right. You'd think that if God were really in charge, He'd fix everyone, so we naturally feel like we have to step in and fix things for Him. Here's a wild hypothesis - what if God really was in charge? Of everything. And He's working with everyone, each in their own way, on His time. And he's got tabs on everyone, and no one is slipping through the cracks, because He's their Shepherd, and a Good Shepherd would never lose a single sheep. Crazy idea, right?

In religion, lifestyle, politics, business, art, in every activity that humans undertake we think we know better than the other guy exactly how it should be done. But we just have to trust that God knows better what others need and is leading them to it like the Good Father he is. It's not my job to correct anyone, it's not my right to correct anyone, and it's impossible to do anyway because I don't have a clue what would be best for them. My only job is to make sure my connection to God is correct, because if it isn't, I've completely lost my life, it's slipped through my fingers. God has given me this amazing life, and I'm just tossing it if I'm disconnected from Him.

Other people's problems are not my problem. The only problem I need to fix is my connection to God. When my connection is strong, if God needs to send me to help others, I'll know exactly how to help them because he's showing me. How do you know if your connection is strong? You're happy. You're in love with life. Everywhere you look you feel surrounded by God's blessings. You don't dislike anyone. Everyone you meet is beautiful to you. God's church is no longer a building for you, it's everywhere you are. The way you're playing is your favorite way to play, and it's fine how everyone else is playing. You're always looking for the beautiful things in life and thanking God for them. You're not confused about what action to take because God is guiding you. You don't worry about what others think of your playing style. But the main way you know that you're playing in God's sandbox is that life is really fun.

Dancing in Hell

Here is a common scenario. Jane is angry because Tarzan didn't do something he said he would do. Jane feels justified in her anger, for Tarzan plainly said that he would swing by the store and pick up some milk on his way home. So she's peeved. Tarzan then gets angry at Jane and feels justified because he got held up at the post office and didn't have time to run Jane's errand. Jane says that if he were better at planning his time, this wouldn't have happened, and she feels justified because Tarzan does have time-management issues. This doesn't sit too well with Tarzan. He feels unfairly accused because he's often running around doing things for Jane and her errands take up his time. So Tarzan gets more angry at her. He yells at her as he grabs the nearest vine and swings away in a huff.

Here's another one. Jack's daughter, Jill, has always been a good, cooperative, obedient daughter - until now. Jill just turned 16 and all the girls are wearing belly-revealing shirts and getting unicorn tattoos on their hips. So Jill wants to do the same. Jack puts his foot down. No daughter of his is going to look like a tramp and get a tattoo like a hoodlum. Jack feels justified in that because when he was growing up, they just had harmless long hair, beads and bell-bottoms, plus, no one had tattoos so why does Jill need one? Jill doesn't appreciate being compared to a tramp and a hoodlum, so she goes out with her girlfriends one night and gets the tattoo against her father's wishes. This infuriates Jack, who feels like he should be able to decide what Jill puts on her body since she's a minor, and legally is under his jurisdiction, so he grounds her and takes away her cell phone. Jill decides not to talk to her father anymore.

One more. Martha is late to work again. George, her supervisor, is at his wit's end. Martha often has trouble finishing the work on her plate and it drives George bananas that in addition to that, she is chronically late. If she doesn't finish her work, he looks bad to his supervisor. Martha, however, sees it differently. She feels she works harder than most people, so even though she can't always keep up with the work load now and then, it's okay. So, who cares if she comes in a few minutes late. But she doesn't say this to George, she just patiently bears her suffering and prays to God to change her boss, like her mother taught her to do. But it's eating her up inside. She's miserable. He's miserable. This goes on for years.

We can change the names and the situations described above and find ourselves in that same dance. We all know the dance well. The dance partners above believe that they are unhappy because the other isn't behaving better so they lash out or brood in an attempt to control the other. They all think that if they can just get the other to shape up, there would be no problem. They each have decided that they won't be happy until the other one mends their ways. It's possible to stay in this dance for an entire lifetime - there's a good definition of hell for you. If the only way you are going to be happy is if you get that other person to act differently, I can say with confidence that you will never be happy. They are never, ever going to do what you want them to do. God made them free.

The only reason we are ever unhappy is because we are demanding happiness from people, things and situations that have zero ability to give us happiness. Happiness never has and never will come from those things. It appears differently, but this is the big lie that everyone has told us and that we come to believe ourselves. It's infuriating, but we can't seem to find our way out of the dance. It seems like the happiness comes from outside you because when they behave better, we do feel better. But tying my happiness to what other people do or don't do is like inviting someone to dance with you in hell. It doesn't matter if you're doing the Twist or the Hustle or the Charleston, you're still in hell, so there's no way the dance is ever going to be fun.

Giving up this hellish dance is possible. God will help you, but you have to let Him. You have to find a way to look at the things that are making you angry, and still be joyful. It seems impossible, doesn't it? But this impossible situation is nothing to God. God makes it all happen. And not only is it possible to do in a relatively short amount of time, it's possible to accomplish with infinitely less effort than we expend in trying to get others to behave. If I align with God, my joy is coming from Him, not the people and things in my world.

It was an illusion anyway that the things outside me ever caused joy, because there is no joy separate from God. If I did feel happiness when someone behaved in a way that pleased me, it was only because I looked at them in a way that opened up my connection to God for a moment. I was appreciating them and seeing what God sees in them. But with God's help, I can train myself to appreciate them and love them and see what God sees in them no matter what they are doing. I can choose to look at them with the unconditional love of a Mother looking at her precious child. No conditions have to be different for me to love them. It just takes a little practice.

I remember the first time I consciously stepped out of the hell-dance. I had been priming the pump consistently for a few weeks, actively looking for God's blessings in my life. At home, at work, on my commute, everywhere I could, I was choosing to look for things that I loved about my life and thanking God for them. I had cut off my contact with newspapers, and television and internet news, and the daily litany of bad things they are so good at digging up. I remember looking up at a beautiful blue sky, and the birds were singing and I breathed in the fresh air. I had practiced looking for His blessings and was finding them everywhere. At that moment I suddenly felt God's joy. It was unmistakable. God was smiling. That night, I got into an argument with my wife. The details of it mean nothing - the important thing was that I was entering the hell-dance and I was so sure I was right. I know I'm right. I have evidence to prove I'm right. A jury of my peers would agree that I'm right. I was also miserable, as I pondered how right I was. Then, since I had been working at finding God's blessings and was a little familiar with what His joy felt like, in contrast it was clear that this felt absolutely horrible. This pain reminded me to say to myself, "Right now, I am separating myself from God, and that is the cause of my pain. My wife's actions are not the cause of my pain." In the next moment I could see that she felt horrible and I could see that her pain also was coming from a separation from God. Not only was it clear that my wife was hurting, but I could no longer hold her responsible for my pain. Suddenly, because I was just a little practiced at seeing God's blessings from working at it for a couple weeks, the magnificent blessing that my wife is made its way into my mind. A second earlier she may as well have had a pitchfork and horns, because I was so certain that she was making my life miserable. But now she suddenly appeared beautiful and radiant, like an angel. Because I was no longer angry at her, she relaxed too, and we talked about how we were both feeling and sorted it out. The dance came to an end.

With such little effort, anyone can do it. I can't say it's not a little hard getting started, but with so very little effort compared to the intense effort we expend in trying to force others to behave, anyone can do it. Once you begin to get the hang of it, something really interesting starts to happen. The people in your life actually start to change, in ways that are pleasing to you. I can only explain it as a gift from God. Once you put your attention on God, He blesses you with ease in your personal relationships. When you don't hold people responsible for your happiness, then just like looking at a child moving through life, whatever others are doing is fine, and you don't feel you have to control them. You enjoy them. You want to serve them. You feel more generous with them and you want them to succeed. They become beautiful to you. You're seeing them with God's eyes.

Your Happiness Is Your Job

Your connection to God is your responsibility, and no one else's. Put another way, your happiness is your responsibility. The moment we say that our happiness depends on what someone else is doing or not doing, we've taken that first step away from God, and are putting our trust in the world instead of Him. My happiness relies 100% on my connection to God, and maintaining that is my business alone.

Conversely, it's not my job to make anyone else happy. Jesus said exactly this when his disciples criticized a woman for anointing His hair with expensive oil, saying that the oil could have been sold and the money given to the poor. He scolded them pretty good; I would have loved to have seen that. Jesus' retort was that the woman was doing the correct thing, worshiping God while she had the opportunity, and not trying to solve the world's problems. But what about Jesus' admonishments to serve the poor? I have to come down on the side of opening up my heart to God first. He'll tell you what to do with your life. If that takes you into soup kitchens, wonderful. But get close to God first, then see where He leads you. He knows just where you are needed and He'll be sure to send you there.

Thinking you have to constantly do for others can be a pretty sticky trap. There are tons of references in the Bible about how we should be taking care of other people, but if you try to do that before lining up with God you're asking for trouble, and people who expect others to make them happy will be drawn to you because you're matching up with their world-view. Look out - those people are never happy, never satisfied. You will never be enough in their eyes. If you're around that dynamic for a long time, you'll start to think you're not enough, too. If this sounds familiar, it's good to learn how to say no, because now you've got more important things to attend to. Tell them you've decided to make a career out of getting close to God, and that they'll just have to wait. God is infinitely better equipped to help them anyway.

How do you know if you're getting close to God? You're joyful. You see the best in people. You naturally enjoy everyone, no matter what they happen to be doing. The world is a beautiful place to you. You have ease in all your relationships. Chaotic people and situations aren't drawn to you. You're laughing a lot. You have clarity about what to do with your time and have plenty of time to accomplish things because you're not putting out fires that started because you acted before you were lined up with Him. You have compassion for people who are being difficult because you know it's painful for them to be disconnected from God. You know that you don't have to make the world a perfect place before you can be happy. You get goose-flesh a lot because you're so joyful to feel His presence. You're not too concerned with getting to where you want to be in life because where you are is really great, but you keep moving forward anyway because God is showing you what to do and where to go. Your mental pain becomes less and less. You stop comparing yourself to others and start paying attention to how much joy you're feeling right now. Joy and God are everything to you.

⚷ Delicious People

Remember how the first blush of love feels? Those first few months of a new relationship are so delicious. When you're apart, you're both so eager to be with each other again and jump back into exploring the world together. When you're in love, you feel great about yourself and you try to show your best side to your new flame. Magically, you can only see the best in them and your new love can do no wrong. You give the other enormous leeway in the relationship, because you love them. If they are a little late, or a little impatient or inattentive, it's nothing to you.

I believe that in those enchanting first days of love we see the world through God's eyes. When we are actively engaged in looking for the best in someone, we are mirroring how God looks at them and that's why it feels so good. I also believe that it's impossible for God to feel bad, and we can be like Him when we are only focused on the best aspects of His children.

After a few months in a new relationship, as the excitement wears off, sometimes we can begin to fall back into our old ways. We lose that effortless ability to see the best in our beloved. Sometimes even the very things that we found cute or adorable can be the same things that begin to bother us as time goes on. Our lover seems to change before our eyes from someone who can do no wrong into a flawed and imperfect person. In reality, our beloved hasn't changed in the least, but the way we look at them does. While it may seem that our joy was coming from that other person, our connection to God was the actual source of that joy we felt. When we find reasons to live in that joy, we tune into where He is. When we actively looked for things we loved in our beloved, we found them, we discovered God in them. Our eyes were full of light.

It's a shame that we lose the energy of those first months of romantic love so soon. For a while, we forget about our problems because our beloved seemed to fill a void in our hearts, but as we return to our routines, our problems are still there. We start looking for something outside ourselves to blame and we can even blame the person who just a few weeks ago seemed to be the cause of so much joy. Fortunately, we can have a second honeymoon not only with our beloved, but with every person in our world. God is there, in them, waiting for us to shine a light on them so we can see them as God sees them, and it only takes the conscious application of attention to their good qualities.

Normally we expect the people and situations in our lives to make us happy without any effort on our part, and we get angry when they don't comply. But we don't have to wait for the people in our lives to change before we can love them. When we see the world through God's eyes, we can fall in love with anybody we run into. Seeing them through God's eyes is as simple as looking for positive qualities in them. The more we do it, the more similar thoughts occur to us, and sooner than you think, you're seeing God's children as He sees them. Then the magnificence, diversity, and astonishing beauty of God's world opens up to us. Every person we encounter becomes delicious to us, and we are hopelessly in love again.

Where Joy Is, God Is

Let's summarize some of the main paths that lead back to the Garden. If you are feeling any kind of mental pain - depression, anger, worry, fear, frustration, jealousy, unworthiness, guilt, any bad-feeling emotion no matter what name you give it - it only means that you are temporarily moving away from God. Not to worry - you know what to do, you want to move towards God. You can tell if you're on track because God is always in the direction of joy.

If nothing is more important to you than walking with God and doing His will, decide that nothing is more important than generating joy, as much as you can, whenever and wherever you can. The quickest, easiest way to generate joy is to make a habit out of constantly appreciating God's blessings in your life. When you take the time to train yourself to proactively look for things that you love about God's awesome creation, it becomes easier and easier until eventually it is effortless. You begin to reach a place where you are in a constant state of praise.

Once you get even a little close to that state of constant praise, that's when the fireworks begin. God's will for your life becomes apparent. The path before you lights up and there is never any confusion about what to do. All your struggles come to an end because God has taken over and is resolving all your problems. Your life is simplified because you only have one job to take care of - that of praising all the ways that God is blessing your life. He does all the rest.

You can begin tonight in bed, before you go to sleep. Give yourself 10 minutes to think about some of God's blessings that will make you happy when you think about them. It can be as simple as you want to make it. As you lay there in bed, you can appreciate the soft pajamas you have, your nice warm bed and clean sheets. Appreciate the light beside your bed, your full belly, remember the beautiful pink sky your wife pointed out at dusk and the marvelous questions your child asked today. Just find something, anything to rejoice about, and soak in the happiness it brings you. Then say to yourself that you're going to sleep well tonight, have good dreams, and wake up ready to start appreciating again. When you wake up, make it your number one job to go through your day seeking out more of God's blessings you can appreciate. Then as you begin finding more and more thoughts like those, it won't be long before you'll be able to peek inside the Garden again.

About the Author

Skye Leith is a writer, puppeteer, actor, teacher, playwright and avid devotee of a variety of religious traditions. His spiritual journey has taken him from his birth religion of Christianity through Native American religions, Bahaism, Vedanta, Judaism, Zen, Tibetan Buddhism and others. *The Key to the Garden* explores the conclusions of this journey within a Christian context. He lives in Nyack, New York with his wife Eileen and his daughter Lazuli.